TRADITIONAL PATCHWORK PATTERNS

FULL-SIZE CUT-OUTS & INSTRUCTIONS FOR 12 QUILTS

CAROL BELANGER GRAFTON

DOVER PUBLICATIONS, INC.
NEW YORK

Published in Canada by General Publishing
Company, Ltd., 30 Lesmill Road, Don Mills,
Toronto, Ontario.
Published in the United Kingdom by Constable
and Company, Ltd., 10 Orange Street, London
WC 2.

"Traditional Patchwork Patterns" is a new
work, first published by Dover Publications,
Inc., in 1974.

International Standard Book Number: 0-486-23015-5
Library of Congress Catalog Card Number: 74-82207

Manufactured in the United States of America
Dover Publications, Inc.
180 Varick Street
New York, N. Y. 10014

INTRODUCTION

The twelve patchwork patterns in this book represent some of the best-loved traditional designs. Most have been selected to provide a good introduction to patchwork quilt making, but a few offer stimulating challenges to more experienced workers. Even more than the novices, those who have already made quilts by copying out designs onto cardboard will appreciate the convenience of the unusual feature of this collection—the carefully designed preprinted cardboard patterns or templates that make up the last half of this publication.

As the title indicates, this work is a collection of immediately useable patterns—not an instruction book on how to do patchwork; that subject is already well covered in numerous inexpensive books (one of the best of which is "The Standard Book of Quilt Making and Collecting" by Marguerite Ickis[1]), and limitations of space permit us only to sketch out the process in brief.

BEGINNING THE QUILT

Kinds of Materials

At the beginning of each pattern, we indicate the amount of 36-inch-wide material you will need to complete a quilt of the specified dimensions. Of course, you are free to revise both the color scheme and the proposed finished size of the quilt; the latter adjustment is accomplished by adding additional blocks or half-blocks to both the width and height, and then adjusting the length of the four border pieces.

The first rule to observe in selecting material for a quilt is to combine the same kinds of fabrics. For instance, linens and cottons go together, silks and satins, and so on. If you want to make a quilt that can be laundered, be sure that ALL the material used is washable and pre-shrunk and that the colors are fast.

For your convenience in sewing, select a soft material, not too closely woven. Closely woven cloth makes the needlework more difficult and is no stronger than thinner goods. Materials that are stiff because of being "treated" with a finish are also difficult to work with. In general, the following materials are good for patchwork quilts: gingham, percale, calico, shirting, broadcloth and cotton-polyester blends.

Cutting Out the Patterns

What could be simpler than to cut the pattern pieces carefully on the dashed lines? Note that these pattern pieces take into consideration the ¼″ seam allowance that is so necessary to patchwork. It is important to keep the edges of the cardboard as neat and firm as possible, so use very sharp, good-sized scissors, a single-edged razor blade or an X-acto knife. Some people prefer to cut out all the pattern pieces pertaining to the design at one time, but novices often cut them out one at a time and then cut the appropriate amount of fabric for each one before working with the next pattern piece.

Making a Sample Block

Always make one block of any pattern before cutting patches for an entire quilt. This gives you the chance to double-check to make sure you like both the pattern and your color choices.

Cutting the Fabric

Cutting is one of the most important steps in making your quilt. You must be accurate in order to have the pattern fit perfectly and to avoid wasting your materials. Have sharp scissors with blades at least 4 inches long. You will need a ruler for marking straight lines, and a pencil with hard lead to avoid blurry marks around the pattern. With these tools at hand, proceed as follows:

1. Press all materials perfectly smooth to eliminate wrinkles.
2. Take one of the cardboard pieces—say Piece No. 1—and refer to the preliminary instructions for the design to find out how many pieces of each fabric you need to complete the quilt. You may want to jot this information down in pencil on the pattern piece itself; i.e., 48 P[ink], 48 G[reen], etc.
3. Next lay one of the cardboard patterns near the top left edge of the material (but not on the selvage), making sure that the long part of the pattern runs parallel with the straight grain of the fabric. Trace around the cardboard with a hard lead pencil.

---

[1]A Dover paperback reprint (0-486-20582-7), 280pp., $3.50.

4. Continue moving the cardboard pattern and tracing it on the fabric the required number of times, moving from left to right, always keeping the long part of the pattern running with the straight grain. Allow at least ⅛″ space between tracings, to make it easier to cut the pieces out.

5. After you have traced the first pattern piece the required number of times, take one of the other pattern pieces that is to be cut from the same material and trace it in a similar manner, again referring to the preliminary instructions to find out the required number of pieces.

6. Carefully cut out the required number of pieces of each color and then organize them according to shape and color. Most people find it convenient to string them together with a single thread running through the center of each (see Figure 1).

7. Even though the fabric requirements have been very carefully calculated it is still a good idea to cut out all the pieces for the entire quilt before one begins to sew, just to make absolutely certain that you have enough material of each color.

Figure 1 STRINGING PATCHES TOGETHER
Run thread through center of patches according to shape and color. Knot at bottom and lift off patch from top as needed.

Marking Seam Allowance

There are at least two accurate methods of marking the ¼″ seam allowance that is so necessary to fitting the pattern pieces together to form blocks.

1. Using a dressmaker's hem gauge or a rule, with a pencil mark the seam allowance on the fabric.

2. Since most fabrics used in quilting are lightweight and semi-transparent, it is often possible to put the cut pieces over the corresponding template and "read" the seam allowance indication, tracing it in pencil on the fabric itself.

Sewing

The simple stitches employed in quilt making are the running stitch (used in piecing parts of the design together and also in quilt stitching) and the hemming stitch (used in appliqué work). See Figure 2.

Use No. 60 thread and a short needle, No. 8. A long needle is not necessary, for very few stitches are taken before drawing the needle through the material. Use white thread unless the patches are cut from very dark cloth. Sew patches together to form blocks, referring to the block diagram that accompanies the preliminary instructions. Use small running stitches to secure each short seam, and then finish with at least two back stitches. The seam should be ¼″ wide and sewn as straight as possible.

Work each block individually and sew several patches together at a time to form a small section of it. Fit sections together to see that the adjoining parts fit exactly. In order to have it perfectly correct, tack corners together with a few over-stitches. Sew the sections together with the usual ¼″ seam.

After you have pieced the block, press it on the wrong side with a warm iron. Press the seams flat—not open.

As for using a sewing machine, old-time quilters frown on anything but the finest hand-sewing when piecing blocks. However, the

Figure 2 RUNNING STITCH
Begin at right, sewing toward left. Knot of thread is on under side of material. In quilting, take stitches about 1/16 inch and space evenly.

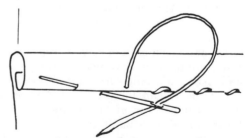

HEMMING STITCH
Sewing from right to left, the needle catches folded edge of hem to the material. Spacing varies according to material.

sewing machine can serve a useful purpose when you are ready to set the blocks together —more about this below.

Setting the Quilt

After you have pieced the required number of blocks, lay them out to get the final effect before setting them together. Check to make sure that each block is turned the proper way, and that the border, if you are using one, fits precisely. As you survey the blocks, keep in mind that they are not yet sewn together and that the seams, when they are finished, will each account for taking up ¼"; of course, this affects the fitting of the border, both as to length and width.

You can now proceed with setting the blocks together. The best way is to join all the blocks of one·row, sewing them with a ¼" seam. Continue joining blocks one row at a time. Some people feel that machine sewing here not only saves time but also strengthens the long seams. Others believe that it is easier to keep the pattern accurate and the corners matched if the work is done by hand. Some hand-sewers also find that the close machine stitches create difficulties later on when one gets ready to do the final quilt stitching.

In sewing on the border strips, begin with the shorter pieces of the top and bottom first. Baste them before stitching. Then handle the side border pieces the same way.

Blocking the Quilt

The term "blocking" means keeping the edges straight on all sides of the quilt so that it will be a perfect rectangle when finished. The term applies to the quilt's divisions and blocks, and also to the border, so the process of blocking is a continuing process from start to finish.

Right at the start, it will help your blocking if you have cut the pieces and blocks according to the warp and weft threads in the material, as we discussed it in the section on Cutting the Fabric. Observance of this rule eliminates the tendency to pucker.

Pull the edges of the block straight with the fingers and pin the corners to the ironing board to hold them rigidly in place. Cover the block with a damp cloth and steam with a warm iron. Do not let the pressing cloth get dry. Press the edges until they are perfectly straight and of equal measurements. The center is pressed last.

It is a good idea to press each block after the sewing is completed. This is also true of the border sections. This means quite a lot of pressing, but it assures greater accuracy in the

final measurements of all units. After the quilt is set together, it will need a final blocking before it is ready to be quilted to the filling and lining.

FINISHING THE QUILT

Quilt Filling and Lining

You should choose the filling for your quilt with the greatest care if you want it to endure for years. It is false economy to use inferior cotton, or wool which has not been properly treated. Your time and painstaking stitching deserve the best material. You may obtain cotton batting that is especially prepared for quilt filling. It comes in large sheets carefully folded and rolled. Perhaps you will need two packages, depending on the size of the quilt.

The back of the quilt is made of lengths of soft material sewn together for correct width

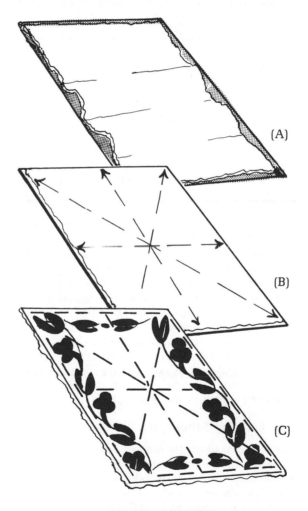

Figure 3 BASTING PROCEDURE
    (A) Placing cotton batting on lining.
    (B) Basting cotton batting to lining.
    (C) Basting top to batting and lining, through center and around edges.

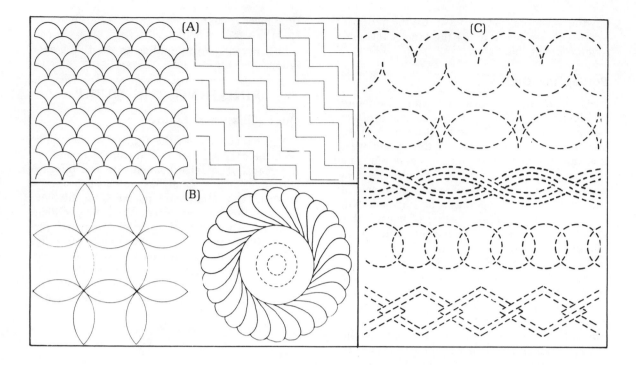

Figure 4 TYPICAL QUILTING DESIGNS
(A) All-over patterns. (B) Decorative patterns for plain blocks. (C) Patterns for narrow strips and borders.

and length. It should be soft and loosely woven to make the quilt stitching easier. The over-all measurements should be 2 inches longer on each side to allow for binding when the quilt is completed. Carefully arrange the lining on a large flat surface, and fasten the corners with thumb tacks. Unroll the cotton batting and spread it out evenly on the lining, making sure there are no lumps or thin places that will make the quilting uneven.

Next, fasten the cotton batting securely to the lining with long basting stitches. Start in the center of the quilt, and sew toward the edge until you have a number of diagonal lines, as shown in Figure 3. You are now ready to lay the neatly pressed top in place over the lining and the cotton filling. Smooth it out and see that the edges correspond on all four sides. The three layers are now basted together just as you basted the first two—in diagonal lines from the center to the edges of the quilt.

The Quilting Stitch

The actual quilt stitching is a simple process for any one who can sew any other form of needlework, but it does take a little practice. The first attempt should be in sitching straight lines, with curves and feathers coming later. It is helpful to use a practice piece of two squares of material with a layer of cotton in between. Try stitching the pieces together with a plain running stitch. You will soon learn the best method of pushing the needle in and out,

and also the direction in which to sew. You will be sure to find that it is easier to sew TOWARD you.

It is an interesting fact that many busy women who enjoy piecing blocks, but who do not care for the final quilting of the three layers, procure the services of professional quilters. There are church organizations, craft shops and private seamstresses who accept quilting at fair rates.

One reason why quilt stitching is often "farmed out" is that it is greatly simplified when done on a quilting frame, which is cumbersome. However, quilting can also be done successfully, if less rapidly, on a quilting hoop.

The purpose of the quilting stitch is to firmly lock the top of the quilt to both its filling and lining. In primitive times, the three layers were held together by stitches at only a few main points, called the counter points or quilt points. Next came interlacing diagonal lines, forming squares and diamonds, then quilt stitching gradually developed into more elaborate designs having a central motif and a border with a "fill-in" space between.

Quilt stitching is used in all kinds of quilts —comforter, appliquéd and patchwork. When the quilt is composed of squares, the quilting stitches cover the plain squares which alternate with the decorated ones, and this gives the effect of throwing the decorated part into more pronounced relief. These quilting stitches in the plain squares are sometimes in straight or diagonal lines and are usually planned to form a contrast to the appliquéd or pieced blocks. Thus, straight lines are chosen to contrast with a curving design, and curves and whirls are chosen when the main pattern is straight or geometrical.

A few popular quilting designs are shown in Figure 4. The pattern that is chosen is traced on the quilt top in chalk in dark-colored areas and in lead pencil in light-colored ones. Use a short SHARP needle, size No. 8-9. The choice of thread should be between Nos. 50 and 70, preferably white. It is important to start the quilting near the center of the frame because it is always easier to sew toward the body. To commence, make a knot at the end of the thread and bring the needle through to the top of the quilt, then pull gently but firmly and the knot will slip through the lower layer into the padding where it will not be seen. To finish off, make a single back stitch and run the thread through the padding. Cut, and the end will be lost.

Binding the Quilt

When the quilting is completed, trim the edges (except the lining extension if used for binding) on all four sides in an even line, being sure to remove any cotton that extends beyond the quilt's top. There are two methods for binding the edges: (1) Make use of the 2-inch extension of the back lining which was left on during the quilting process. Even it off all around, turn up an edge for a seam, and fold up over the top of the quilt. Sew in place with small hemming stitches in matching color thread. (2) Bind the edges with bias strips, if you are going to use a binding of different color or a scalloped border. Cut the bias strips 1 inch wide and sew them together. The binding is done by laying the bias strip along the outside edge of the quilt, and fitting the edges together so they match exactly. Sew the bias strip and all three layers together with a ¼-inch seam, using a running stitch. After the sewing is done, turn the quilt over and turn down the edges of the bias strip ¼ inch. Fold this over the back of the quilt and sew securely to the bottom layer with small hemming stitches.

RIBBON BORDER QUILT

SIZE OF QUILT

This quilt, measuring 78 x 96 inches, is made up of eighty 9-inch pieced blocks set eight in width and ten in length with a 3-inch plain border.

NUMBER OF PIECES TO BE CUT

NOTE: Cut strips first to get full length without piecing.

Piece No. 1.........160 Pink
Piece No. 2.........160 White
Piece No. 2.........160 Light Green
Piece No. 3......... 80 Light Green
Piece No. 3......... 80 White
Piece No. 3.........320 Blue

2 strips, 3½ x 78½ inches ....Pink
2 strips, 3½ x 96½ inches ....Pink

AMOUNT OF MATERIAL

White ....1½ yards
Blue 3   yards
Light Green ....1½ yards
Pink ....5½ yards

SPECIAL INSTRUCTIONS

When sewing the blocks together, let the large center "V" point downward in the first row, upward in the second row, downward in the third row, etc., to obtain the overall design shown on the facing page.

COLOR CHART

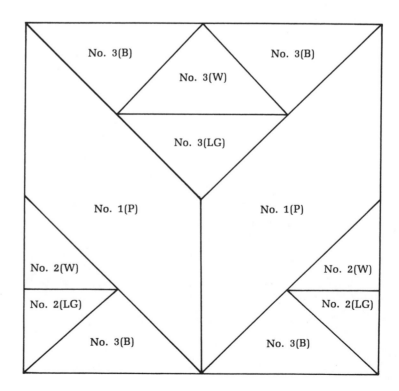

LEGEND

(B) — Blue
(W) — White
(LG) — Light Green
(P) — Pink

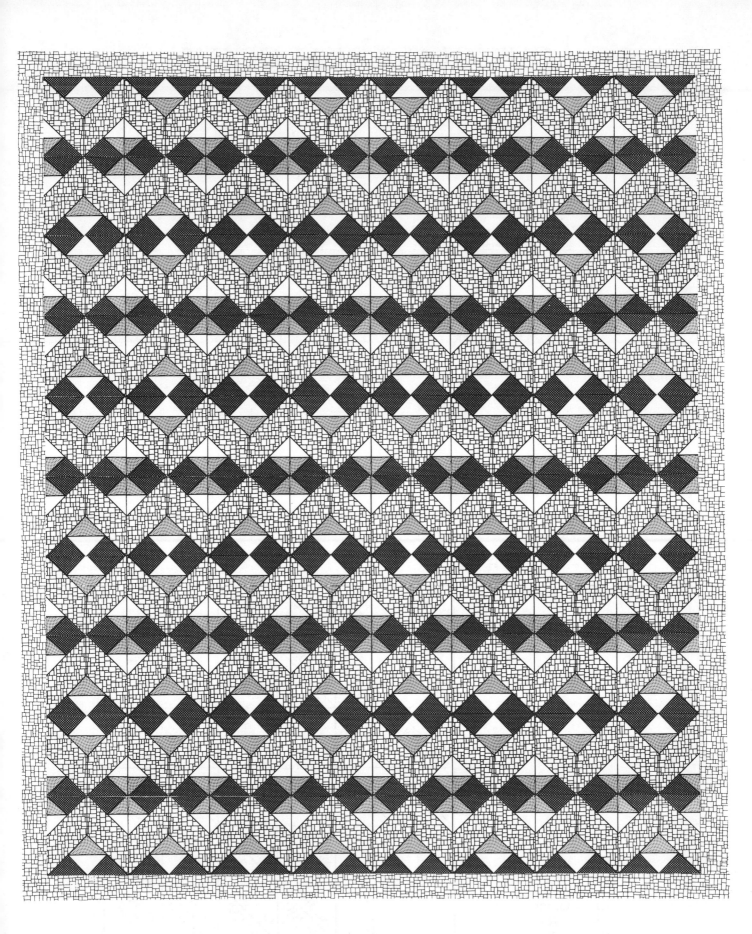

Patterns for this quilt are given on page 27.

3

CUT GLASS DISH QUILT

SIZE OF QUILT

This quilt, measuring 81 x 96 inches, is made up of thirty 15-inch pieced blocks set five in width and six in length with a 3-inch plain border.

NUMBER OF PIECES TO BE CUT

NOTE: Cut strips first to get full length without piecing.

Piece No. 1 . . . . 720 White
Piece No. 1 . . . . 720 Orange
Piece No. 2 . . . . 90 Yellow

2 strips, 3½ x 81½ inches . . . . . Orange
2 strips, 3½ x 96½ inches . . . . . Orange

AMOUNT OF MATERIAL

White 3   yards
Yellow . . . . 4½ yards
Orange . . . . 5½ yards

COLOR CHART

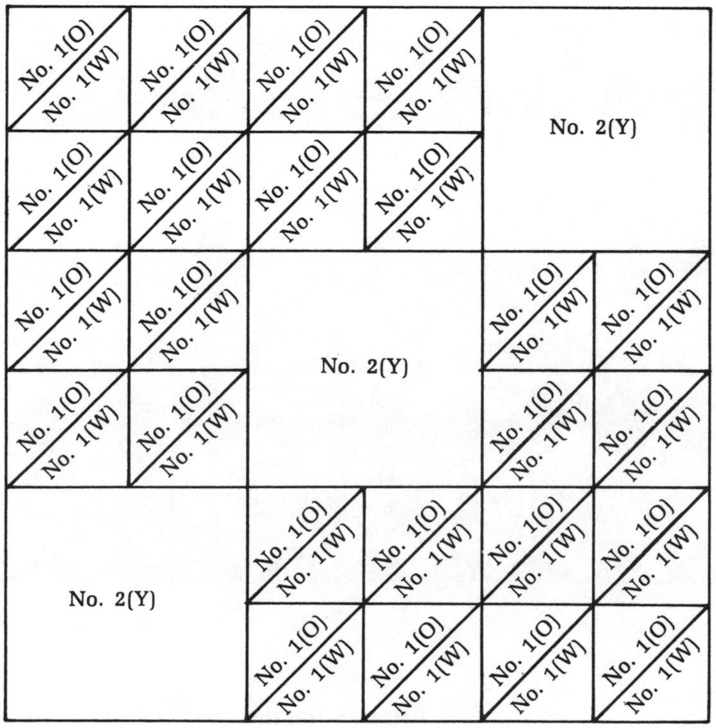

LEGEND

(O) — Orange
(W) — White
(Y) — Yellow

4

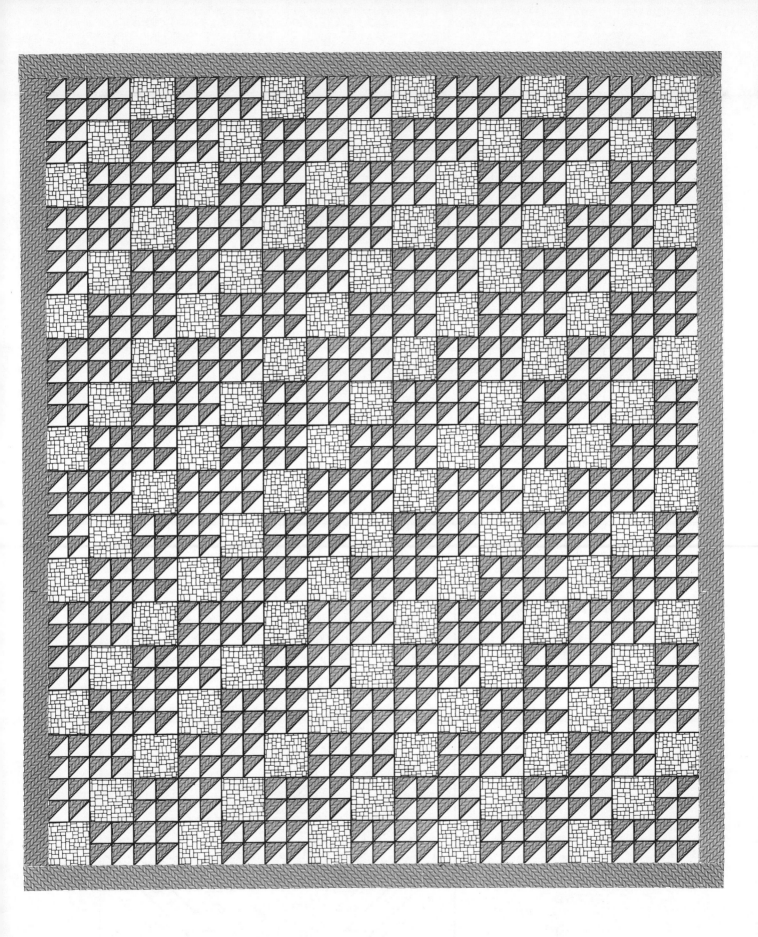

Patterns for this quilt are given on page 29.

PINEAPPLE QUILT

SIZE OF QUILT

This quilt, measuring 63 x 82 inches, is made of twelve 19-inch blocks set three in width and four in length and a 3-inch plain border. The pieces of this pattern are appliqued on plain 19-inch white squares.

NUMBER OF PIECES TO BE CUT

NOTE: Cut strips first to get full length without piecing.

Piece No. 1 . . . . 48 Green
Piece No. 2 . . . . 48 Yellow
Piece No. 3 . . . . 48 Yellow
Piece No. 4 . . . . 48 Yellow
Piece No. 5 . . . . 48 Yellow
Piece No. 6 . . . . 48 Yellow
Piece No. 7 . . . . 48 Yellow
Piece No. 8 . . . . 48 Yellow

2 strips, 3½ x 63½ inches . . . . . . Green
2 strips, 3½ x 82½ inches . . . . . . Green
12 squares, 19½ x 19½ inches . . . . White

AMOUNT OF MATERIAL

White . . . . 3 yards
Yellow . . . . 2 yards and 24 inches
Green . . . . 2 yards and 24 inches

SPECIAL INSTRUCTIONS

Crease white foundation block diagonally in each direction. Crease all the pieces, after cutting, through center as indicated on pattern. Sew pieces 1, 2, 3, 4, 5, 6 and 7 together, matching center crease. Lay pieced section on foundation block, and applique, once again matching the crease. Applique piece No. 8 on separately, matching crease of No. 7 and foundation block.

COLOR CHART

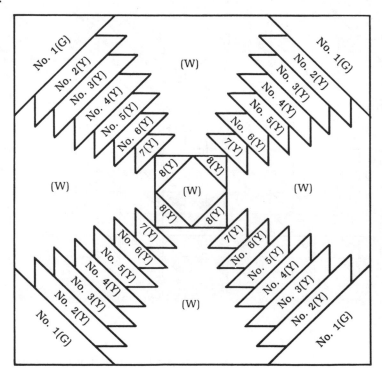

LEGEND

(G) — Green
(Y) — Yellow

6

Patterns for this quilt are given on pages 31 and 33.

7

CUBE WORK QUILT

SIZE OF QUILT

This quilt, measuring 78 x 100 inches, is made up of forty-eight pieced blocks, each of which measures 13 inches wide by 12½ inches deep. The blocks are set six in width and eight in length.

NUMBER OF PIECES TO BE CUT

Piece No. 1............... 96 White
Piece No. 2............... 96 White
Piece No. 3.............288 Print
Piece No. 3.............288 Yellow
Piece No. 3.............288 Green
Piece No. 4.............. 96 White
Piece No. 5.............192 White

AMOUNT OF MATERIAL

White ....4 yards
Print ....2 yards and 9 inches
Yellow ....2 yards and 9 inches
Green ....2 yards and 9 inches

COLOR CHART

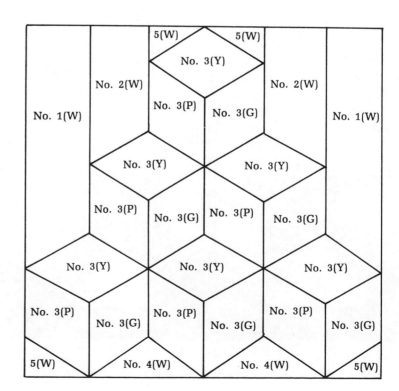

LEGEND

(W) — White
(P) — Print
(Y) — Yellow
(G) — Green

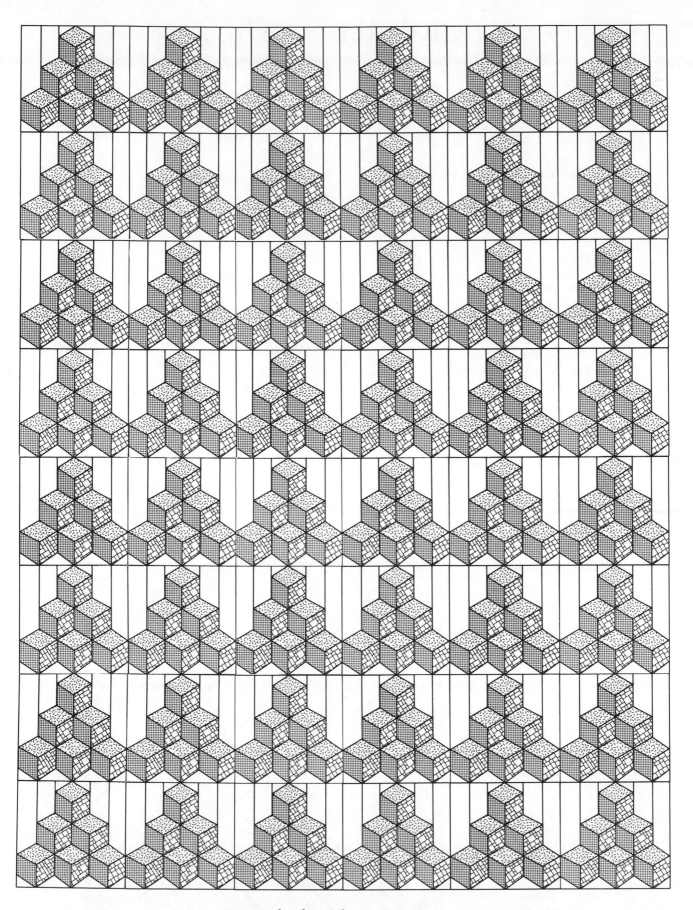

Patterns for this quilt are given on page 35.

ROCKY GLEN QUILT

SIZE OF QUILT

This quilt, measuring 81 x 93½ inches, is made up of forty-two 12½-inch pieced blocks set six in width and seven in length with a 3-inch plain border.

NUMBER OF PIECES TO BE CUT

NOTE: Cut strips first to get full length without piecing.

Piece No. 1 . . . . 84 Blue
Piece No. 2 . . . . 168 Pink
Piece No. 3 . . . . 294 Blue
Piece No. 3 . . . . 168 Pink
Piece No. 3 . . . . 336 White
Piece No. 4 . . . . 672 White
Piece No. 5 . . . . 168 White

2 strips, 3½ x 81½ inches . . . . . . .Blue
2 strips, 3½ x 94 inches . . . . .Blue

AMOUNT OF MATERIAL

White .3 yards
Pink .3 yards
Blue .4½ yards

COLOR CHART

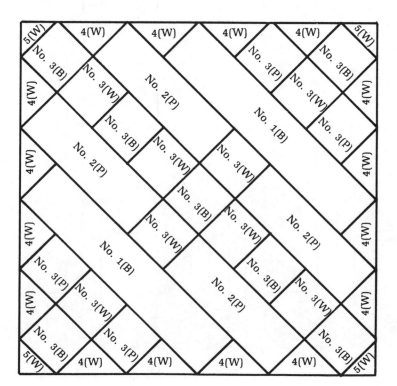

LEGEND

(B) — Blue
(P) — Pink
(W) — White

Patterns for this quilt are given on page 37.

TREE OF PARADISE QUILT

SIZE OF QUILT

This quilt, measuring 80 x 106 inches, is made up of eighteen 18-inch pieced blocks, ten large and four small plain triangles, and a 2-inch plain border.

NUMBER OF PIECES TO BE CUT

NOTE: Cut triangles and strips first to get full length without piecing.

Piece No. 1 . . . . 36 White
Piece No. 1 . . . . 18 Brown
Piece No. 1 . . . . 18 Green
Piece No. 2 . . . . 18 Brown
Piece No. 3 . . . . 54 Tan
Piece No. 4 . . . . .540 Tan
Piece No. 4 . . . . .648 Green
Piece No. 5 . . . . 36 White
Piece No. 6 . . . . 36 Brown

10 triangles (one-half of
   18-inch squares) . . . . .White
4 triangles (one-fourth of
   18-inch triangles) . . . . .White
2 strips, 2½ x 80½ inches . . . . . .Brown
2 strips, 2½ x 106½ inches . . . . .Brown

AMOUNT OF MATERIAL

White . . . . .5 yards
Brown . . . . . . .2 yards and 24 inches
Tan . . . . .2 yards
Green . . . . .2 yards and 24 inches

COLOR CHART

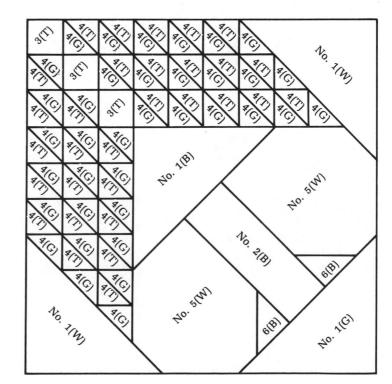

LEGEND

(W) — White
(B) — Brown
(G) — Green
(T) — Tan

Patterns for this quilt are given on pages 39 and 41.

STARLIGHT QUILT

SIZE OF QUILT

This quilt, measuring 83 x 98 inches, is made up of thirty 15-inch pieced blocks set five in width and six in length with a 4-inch border.

NUMBER OF PIECES TO BE CUT

NOTE: Cut strips first to get full length without piecing.

Piece No. 1 . . . . 240 White
Piece No. 2 . . . . 240 White
Piece No. 3 . . . . 120 Blue
Piece No. 3 . . . . 120 Light Blue
Piece No. 4 . . . . 240 Blue
Piece No. 5 . . . . 60 Blue
Piece No. 5 . . . . 60 Light Blue

2 strips, 4½ x 83½ inches . . . . Blue
2 strips, 4½ x 98½ inches . . . . Blue

AMOUNT OF MATERIAL

White . . . . 6 yards
Blue . . . . 4½ yards
Light Blue . . . . . 2 yards

COLOR CHART

LEGEND

(W) — White
(B) — Blue
(LB) — Light Blue

14

Patterns for this quilt are given on page 43.

DOUBLE IRISH CHAIN QUILT

SIZE OF QUILT

This quilt, measuring 80 x 100 inches, is made of twenty 20-inch pieced blocks set four in width and five in length.

NUMBER OF PIECES TO BE CUT

Piece No. 1.............. 40 White
Piece No. 2..............160 White
Piece No. 3..............520 White
Piece No. 3..............640 Green

AMOUNT OF MATERIAL

White ....6 yards
Green ....3½ yards

COLOR CHART

3(W)	3(G)	3(W)	3(G)	3(W)	3(G)	No. 2(W)		3(G)
3(G)	3(W)	3(G)	3(W)	3(G)				
3(W)	3(G)	3(W)	3(G)	3(W)	No. 2(W)	No. 1(W)		No. 2(W)
3(G)	3(W)	3(G)	3(W)	3(G)				
3(W)	3(G)	3(W)	3(G)	3(W)	3(G)	No. 2(W)		3(G)
3(G)	No. 2(W)			3(G)	3(W)	3(G)	3(W)	3(G)	3(W)
No. 2(W)	No. 1(W)			No. 2(W)	3(G)	3(W)	3(G)	3(W)	3(G)
					3(W)	3(G)	3(W)	3(G)	3(W)
					3(G)	3(W)	3(G)	3(W)	3(G)
3(G)	No. 2(W)			3(G)	3(W)	3(G)	3(W)	3(G)	3(W)

LEGEND

(W) — White
(G) — Green

16

Patterns for this quilt are given on page 45.

BLEEDING HEART QUILT

SIZE OF QUILT

This quilt, measuring 84 x 96 inches, is made up of thirty 12-inch pieced blocks (set five in width and six in length) surrounded by a border composed of four additional blocks (one at each corner) and four 12-inch-wide strips with applique.

NUMBER OF PIECES TO BE CUT

NOTES: Cut scallops and strips first to get full length without piecing. Sixteen of the Deep Pink No. 2 pieces are used in the border.

Piece No. 1............136 White
Piece No. 2............154 Deep Pink
Piece No. 3............272 White
Piece No. 4............136 Green
Piece No. 5............136 White
Piece No. 6............ 34 Green

Scallops .... 22 Green
2 strips, 12½ x 61 inches ....White
2 strips, 12½ x 73 inches ....White

AMOUNT OF MATERIAL

White ....7 yards and 15 inches
Deep Pink .....2 yards and 9 inches
Green ....2 yards and 12 inches

COLOR CHART

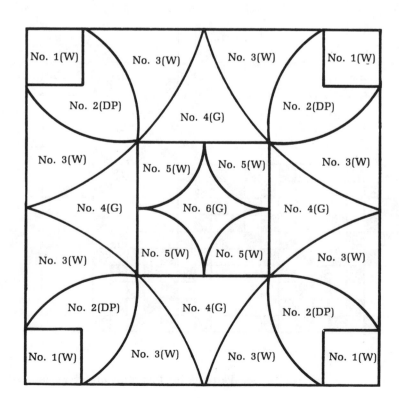

LEGEND

(W) — White
(DP) — Deep Pink
(G) — Green

18

Patterns for this quilt are given on pages 47 and 49.

BARRISTER'S BLOCK QUILT

SIZE OF QUILT

This quilt, measuring 78 x 96 inches, is made up of sixteen 18-inch pieced blocks and eight half blocks. (There is a row of half blocks at the top and one at the bottom of the quilt.) The edge is finished with a 3-inch plain border.

NUMBER OF PIECES TO BE CUT

NOTE: Cut strips first in order to get full length without piecing.

Piece No. 1............240 Light Blue
Piece No. 1............240 Dark Blue
Piece No. 1............320 White
Piece No. 2............ 80 White
Piece No. 3............ 40 Light Blue
Piece No. 3............ 40 Dark Blue
Piece No. 3............ 80 White
Piece No. 4............ 80 White

2 strips, 3½ x 78½ inches....Dark Blue
2 strips, 3½ x 96½ inches....Dark Blue

AMOUNT OF MATERIAL

White ....6 yards
Light Blue .....2 yards and 24 inches
Dark Blue .....4 yards and 12 inches

SPECIAL INSTRUCTIONS

When sewing blocks together, place them to obtain the design shown opposite, with white squares at the intersections of four blocks.

COLOR CHART

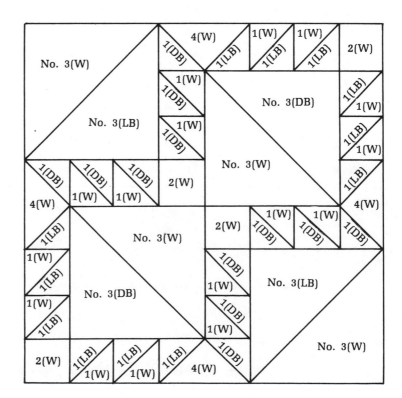

LEGEND

(LB) — Light Blue
(DB) — Dark Blue
(W) — White

20

Patterns for this quilt are given on page 51.

BUTTERCUP QUILT

SIZE OF QUILT

This quilt, measuring 78 x 90 inches, is made up of one hundred sixty-eight 6-inch pieced blocks set twelve in width and fourteen in length. The edge of the quilt is formed by half blocks. Fifty-two of these half blocks are required. Four one-quarter blocks are needed for the corners.

NUMBER OF PIECES TO BE CUT

Piece No. 1.......780 Light Green
Piece No. 2.......780 Yellow or Print
Piece No. 3.......780 White

AMOUNT OF MATERIAL

Green ....4 yards and 12 inches
Yellow or Print.4 yards and 30 inches
White ....3 yards and 24 inches

COLOR CHART

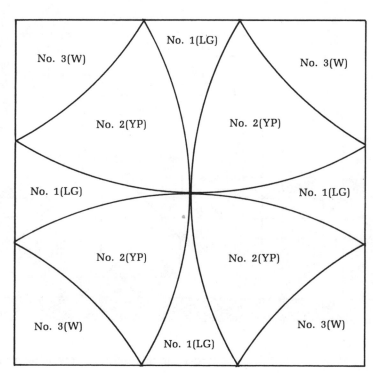

LEGEND

(LG) — Light Green
(YP) — Yellow or Print
(W) — White

22

Patterns for this quilt are given on page 53.

INTERLACED BLOCKS QUILT

SIZE OF QUILT

This quilt, measuring 72 x 87 inches, is made up of twenty 15-inch pieced blocks set four in width and five in length with a 6-inch plain border.

NUMBER OF PIECES TO BE CUT

NOTE: Cut strips first to get full length without piecing.

Piece No. 1 . . . . 80 Dark Blue
Piece No. 2 . . . . 40 White
Piece No. 2 . . . . 20 Medium Blue
Piece No. 3 . . . . 40 Medium Blue
Piece No. 4 . . . . 20 Medium Blue
Piece No. 4 . . . . 20 White
Piece No. 5 . . . . 20 Light Blue
Piece No. 5 . . . . 40 White
Piece No. 6 . . . . 60 White
Piece No. 6 . . . . 20 Light Blue
Piece No. 7 . . . . .100 White
Piece No. 7 . . . . 20 Medium Blue
Piece No. 7 . . . . .100 Light Blue

2 strips, 6½ x 72½ inches . . . . . . White
2 strips, 6½ x 87½ inches . . . . . . White

AMOUNT OF MATERIAL

White .6½ yards
Dark Blue . . . . .2 yards
Light Blue . . . . .2 yards
Medium Blue . . . . .2 yards

COLOR CHART

LEGEND

(DB) — Dark Blue
(W) — White
(MB) — Medium Blue
(LB) — Light Blue

Patterns for this quilt are given on pages 55 and 57.

PATTERN PIECES FOR
RIBBON BORDER QUILT

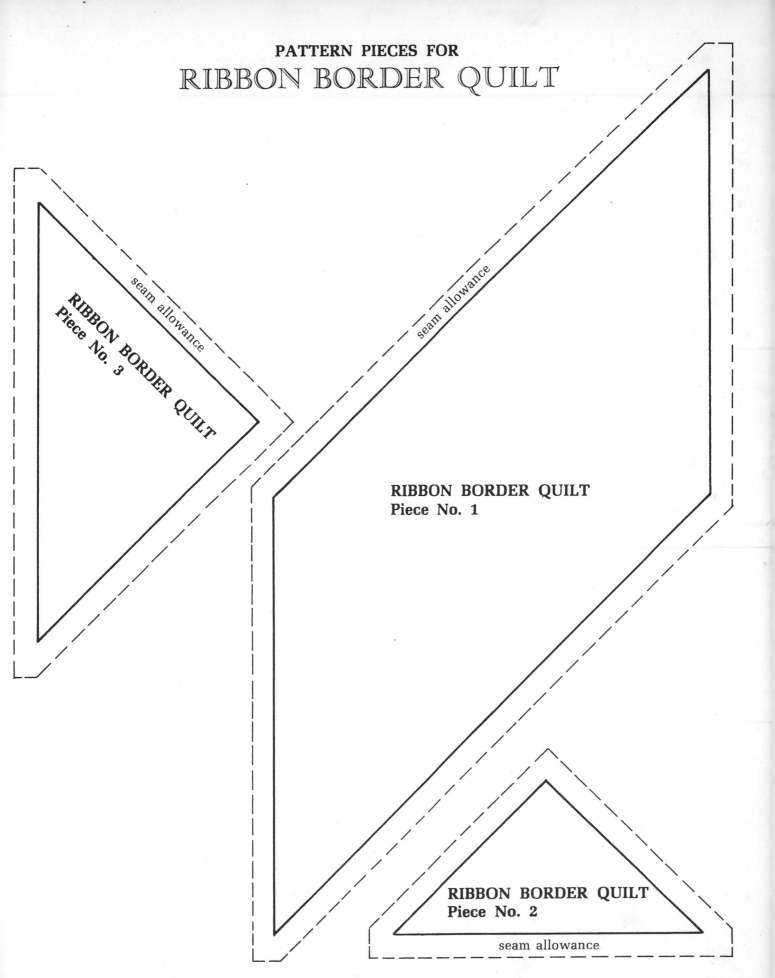

seam allowance

seam allowance

RIBBON BORDER QUILT
Piece No. 3

RIBBON BORDER QUILT
Piece No. 1

RIBBON BORDER QUILT
Piece No. 2

seam allowance

CUT GLASS DISH QUILT

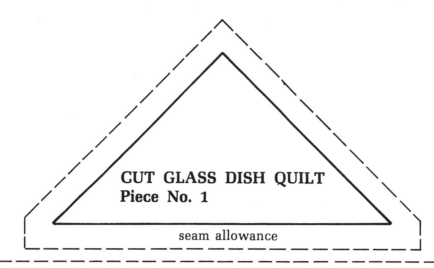

CUT GLASS DISH QUILT
Piece No. 1

seam allowance

CUT GLASS DISH QUILT
Piece No. 2

seam allowance

PINEAPPLE QUILT

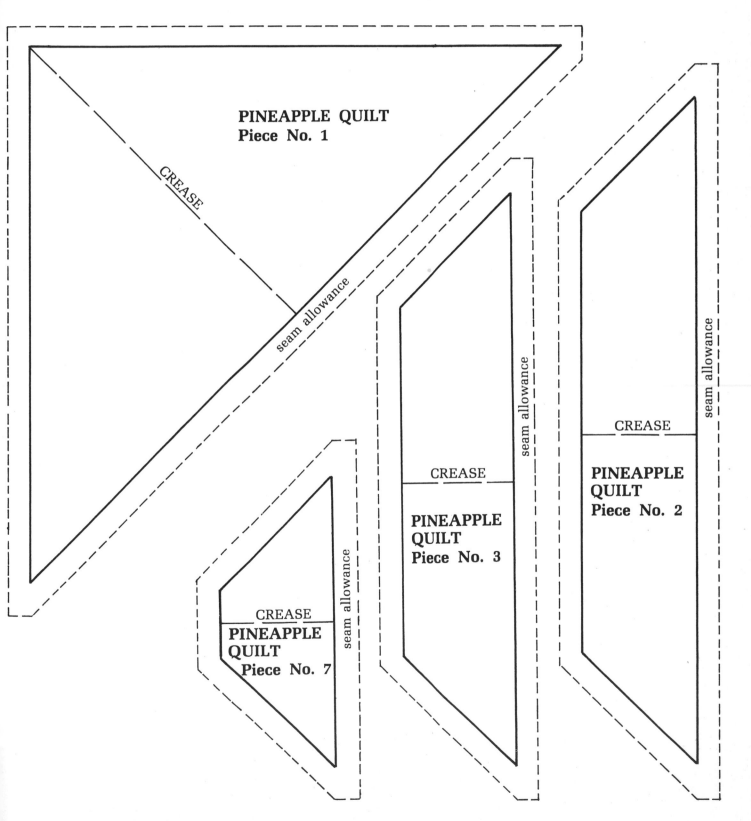

PINEAPPLE QUILT
Piece No. 1

CREASE

seam allowance

CREASE

seam allowance

PINEAPPLE QUILT
Piece No. 2

CREASE

PINEAPPLE
QUILT
Piece No. 3

seam allowance

CREASE
PINEAPPLE
QUILT
Piece No. 7

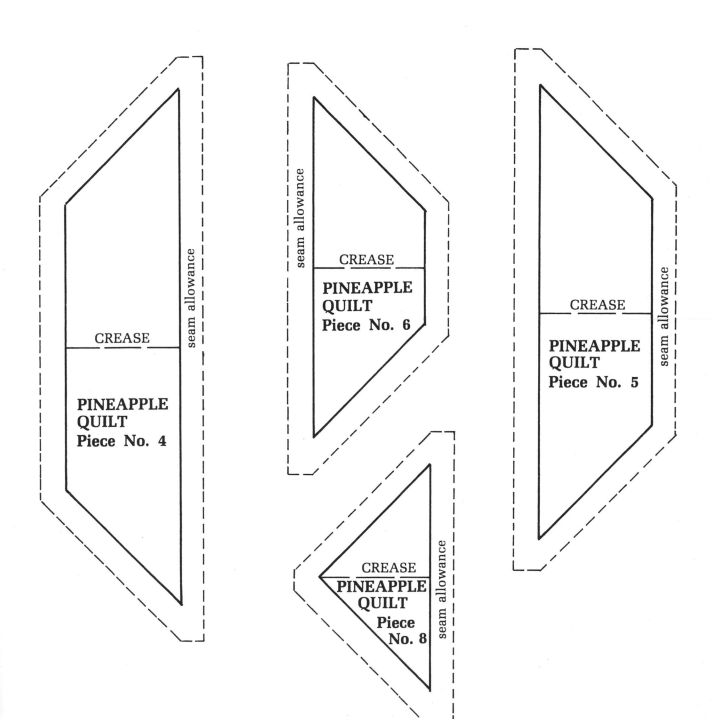

seam allowance

CREASE

**PINEAPPLE
QUILT
Piece No. 4**

seam allowance

CREASE

**PINEAPPLE
QUILT
Piece No. 6**

CREASE

**PINEAPPLE
QUILT
Piece No. 5**

seam allowance

CREASE
**PINEAPPLE
QUILT
Piece
No. 8**

seam allowance

CUBE WORK QUILT

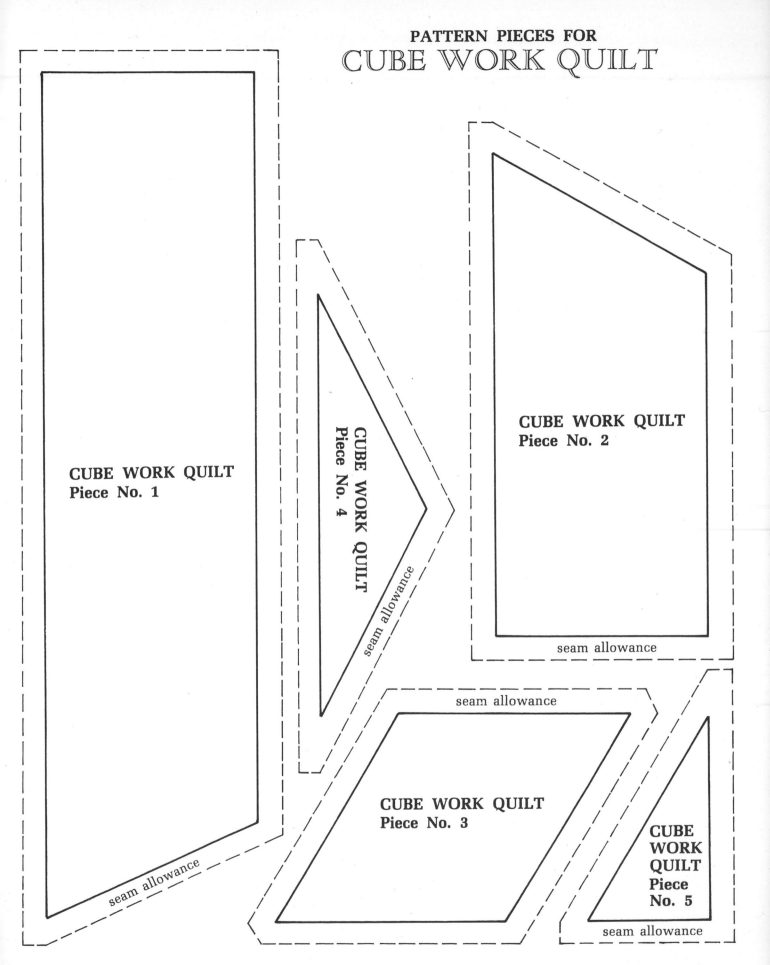

CUBE WORK QUILT
Piece No. 1

CUBE WORK QUILT
Piece No. 4

CUBE WORK QUILT
Piece No. 2

seam allowance

seam allowance

seam allowance

CUBE WORK QUILT
Piece No. 3

CUBE
WORK
QUILT
Piece
No. 5

seam allowance

seam allowance

ROCKY GLEN QUILT
Piece No. 1

NOTE: THIS IS ONE-HALF OF PIECE NO. 1. PLACE ON FOLD OF MATERIAL WHERE INDICATED.

PLACE ON FOLD OF MATERIAL

seam allowance

ROCKY GLEN QUILT
Piece No. 2

seam allowance

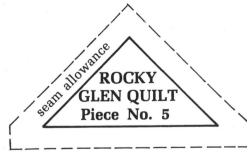

ROCKY GLEN QUILT
Piece No. 5

seam allowance

ROCKY GLEN QUILT
Piece No. 3

seam allowance

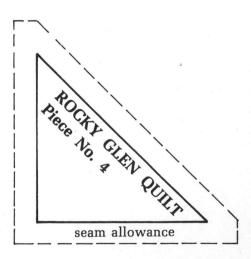

ROCKY GLEN QUILT
Piece No. 4

seam allowance

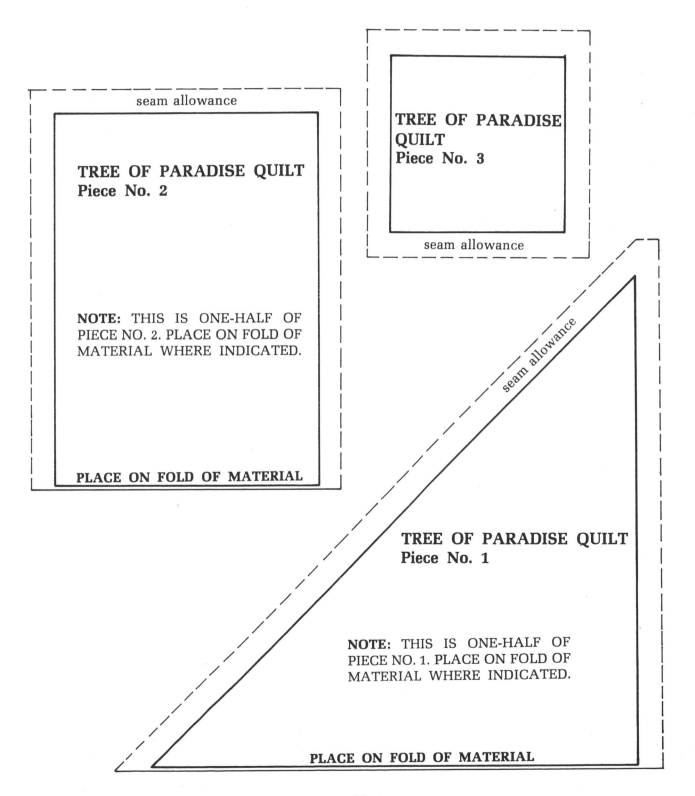

seam allowance

TREE OF PARADISE QUILT
Piece No. 2

NOTE: THIS IS ONE-HALF OF PIECE NO. 2. PLACE ON FOLD OF MATERIAL WHERE INDICATED.

PLACE ON FOLD OF MATERIAL

TREE OF PARADISE QUILT
Piece No. 3

seam allowance

seam allowance

TREE OF PARADISE QUILT
Piece No. 1

NOTE: THIS IS ONE-HALF OF PIECE NO. 1. PLACE ON FOLD OF MATERIAL WHERE INDICATED.

PLACE ON FOLD OF MATERIAL

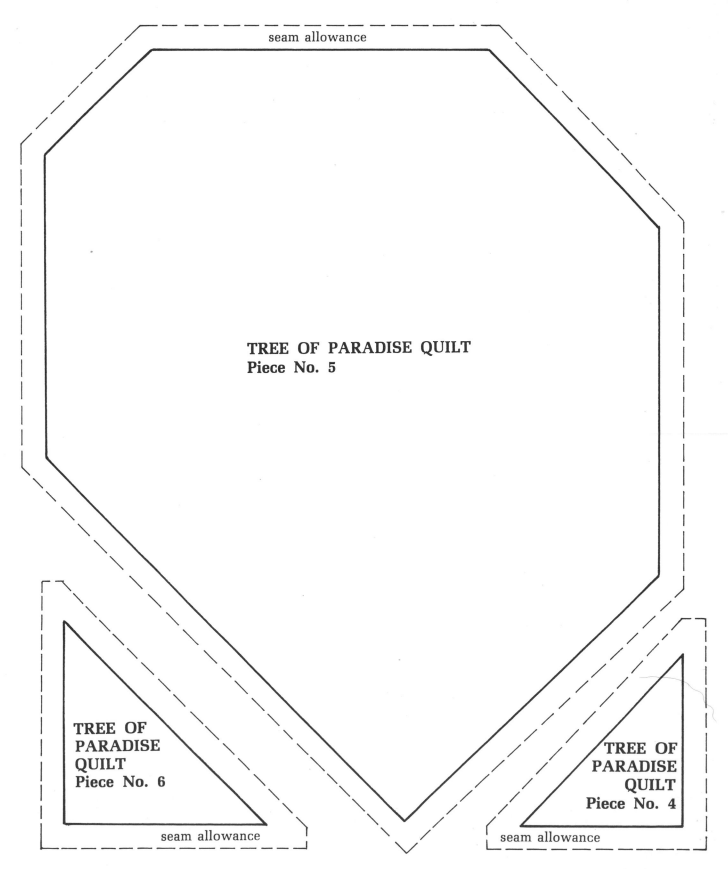

seam allowance

TREE OF PARADISE QUILT
Piece No. 5

TREE OF PARADISE QUILT
Piece No. 6

TREE OF PARADISE QUILT
Piece No. 4

seam allowance

seam allowance

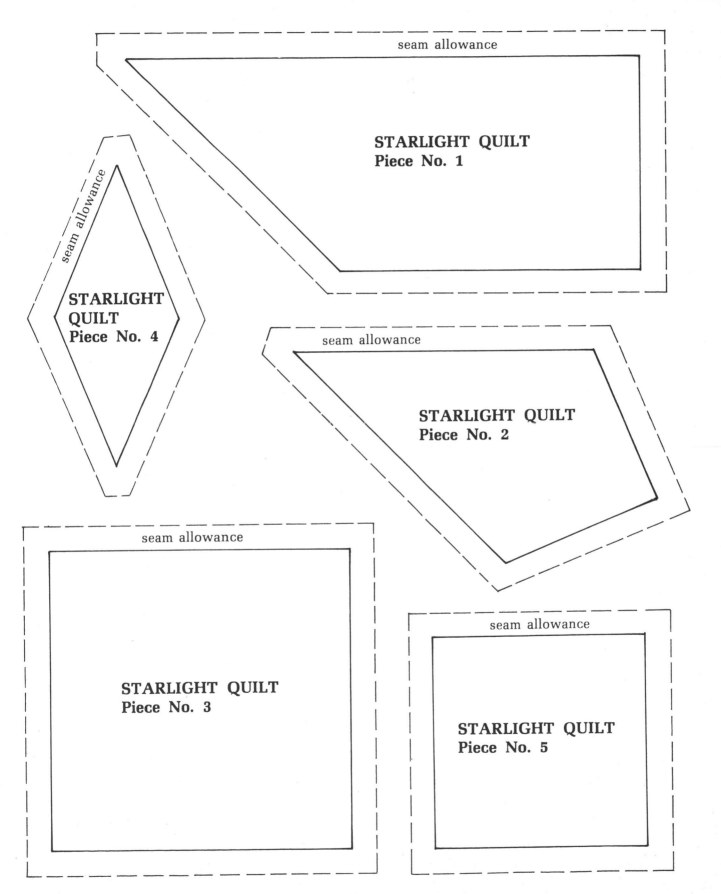

seam allowance

STARLIGHT QUILT
Piece No. 1

seam allowance

STARLIGHT QUILT Piece No. 4

seam allowance

STARLIGHT QUILT
Piece No. 2

seam allowance

STARLIGHT QUILT
Piece No. 3

seam allowance

STARLIGHT QUILT
Piece No. 5

DOUBLE IRISH CHAIN QUILT

seam allowance

DOUBLE IRISH CHAIN QUILT
Piece No. 1

NOTE: THIS IS ONE-HALF OF
PIECE NO. 1. PLACE ON FOLD OF
MATERIAL WHERE INDICATED.

PLACE ON FOLD OF MATERIAL

seam allowance

DOUBLE IRISH CHAIN QUILT
Piece No. 2

**DOUBLE IRISH CHAIN
QUILT**
Piece No. 3

seam allowance

BLEEDING HEART QUILT

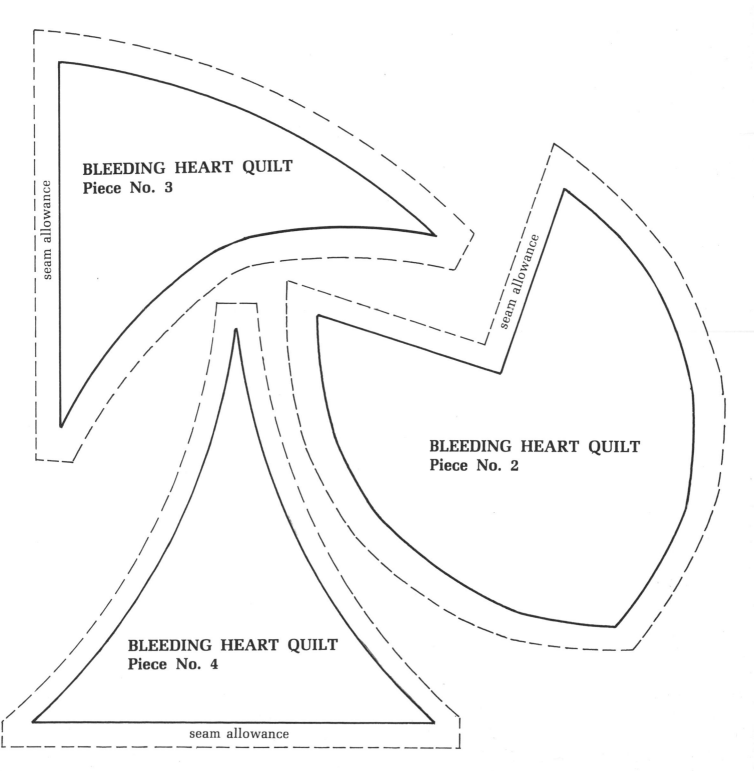

BLEEDING HEART QUILT
Piece No. 3

seam allowance

BLEEDING HEART QUILT
Piece No. 2

seam allowance

BLEEDING HEART QUILT
Piece No. 4

seam allowance

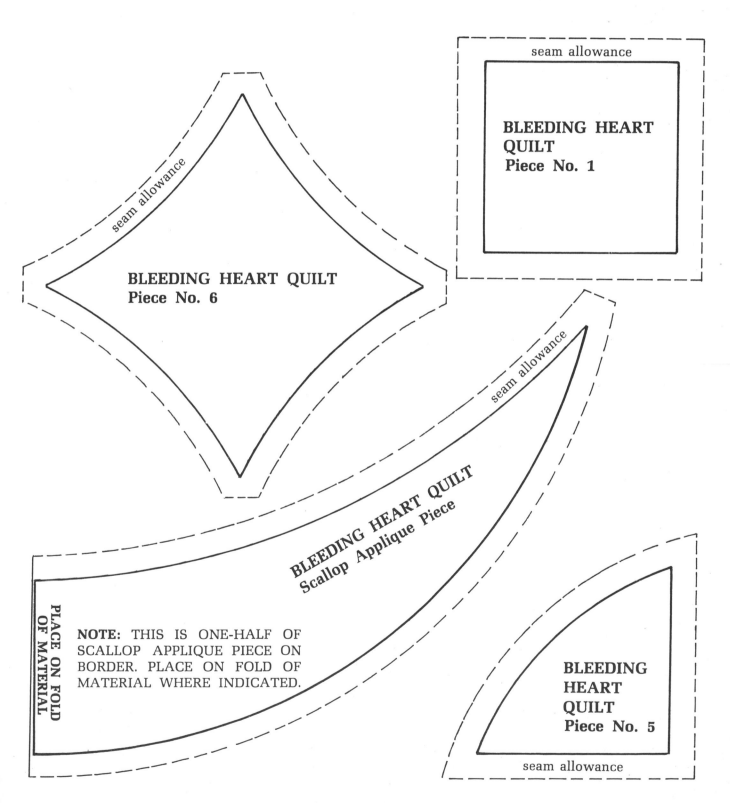

seam allowance

BLEEDING HEART
QUILT
Piece No. 1

seam allowance

BLEEDING HEART QUILT
Piece No. 6

BLEEDING HEART QUILT
Scallop Applique Piece

seam allowance

PLACE ON FOLD
OF MATERIAL

NOTE: THIS IS ONE-HALF OF
SCALLOP APPLIQUE PIECE ON
BORDER. PLACE ON FOLD OF
MATERIAL WHERE INDICATED.

BLEEDING
HEART
QUILT
Piece No. 5

seam allowance

BARRISTER'S BLOCK QUILT

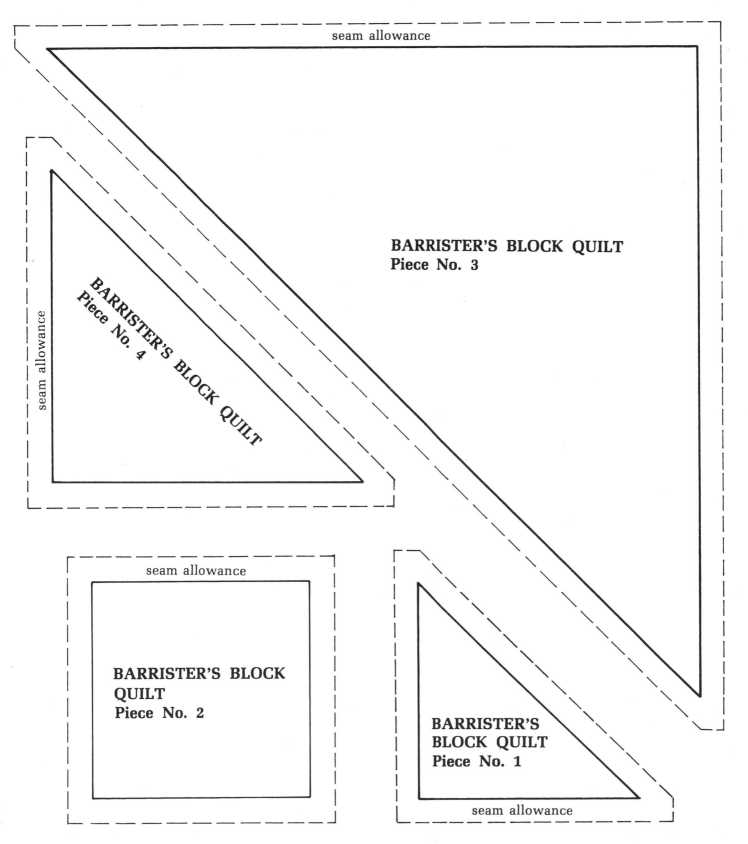

seam allowance

BARRISTER'S BLOCK QUILT
Piece No. 3

seam allowance

seam allowance

BARRISTER'S BLOCK QUILT
Piece No. 4

seam allowance

BARRISTER'S BLOCK
QUILT
Piece No. 2

BARRISTER'S
BLOCK QUILT
Piece No. 1

seam allowance

BUTTERCUP QUILT

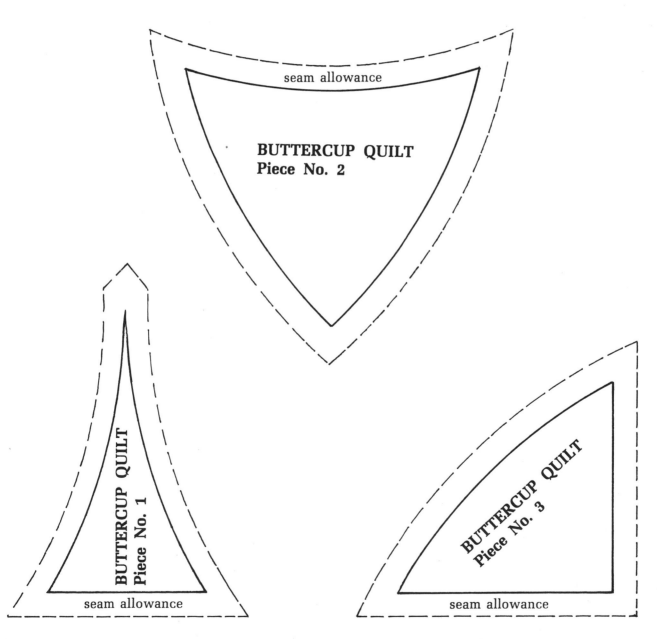

seam allowance

BUTTERCUP QUILT
Piece No. 2

BUTTERCUP QUILT
Piece No. 1

seam allowance

BUTTERCUP QUILT
Piece No. 3

seam allowance

INTERLACED BLOCKS QUILT

seam allowance

INTERLACED BLOCKS QUILT
Piece No. 1

NOTE: THIS IS ONE-HALF OF PIECE NO. 1. PLACE ON FOLD OF MATERIAL WHERE INDICATED.

PLACE ON FOLD OF MATERIAL

seam allowance

INTERLACED BLOCKS QUILT
Piece No. 2

NOTE: THIS IS ONE-HALF OF PIECE NO. 2. PLACE ON FOLD OF MATERIAL WHERE INDICATED.

PLACE ON FOLD OF MATERIAL

seam allowance

INTERLACED BLOCKS QUILT
Piece No. 3

seam allowance

**INTERLACED
BLOCKS
QUILT
Piece No. 7**

seam allowance

**INTERLACED BLOCKS QUILT
Piece No. 4**

seam allowance

**INTERLACED BLOCKS QUILT
Piece No. 5**

seam allowance

**INTERLACED BLOCKS QUILT
Piece No. 6**